Note to Pa.

DK READERS is a compelling program for beginning readers, designed in conjunction with leading literacy experts, including Dr. Linda Gambrell, Distinguished Professor of Education at Clemson University. Dr. Gambrell has served as President of the National Reading Conference, the College Reading Association, and the International Reading Association.

Beautiful illustrations and superb full-color photographs combine with engaging, easy-to-read stories to offer a fresh approach to each subject in the series. Each DK READER is guaranteed to capture a child's interest while developing his or her reading skills, general knowledge, and love of reading.

The five levels of DK READERS are aimed at different reading abilities, enabling you to choose the books that are exactly right for your child:

Pre-level 1: Learning to read
Level 1: Beginning to read
Level 2: Beginning to read alone
Level 3: Reading alone
Level 4: Proficient readers

The "normal" age at which a child begins to read can be anywhere from three to eight years old. Adult participation through the lower levels is very helpful for providing encouragement, discussing storylines, and sounding out unfamiliar words.

No matter which level you select, you can be sure that you are helping your child learn to read, then read to learn!

LONDON, NEW YORK, MUNICH,
MELBOURNE, and DELHI

DK LONDON
Series Editor Deborah Lock
US Senior Editor Shannon Beatty
Project Art Editor Hoa Luc
Production Editor Francesca Wardell

Reading Consultant
Linda Gambrell, Ph.D.

DK DELHI
Editor Nandini Gupta
Assistant Art Editor Yamini Panwar
DTP Designer Anita Yadav
Picture Researcher Aditya Katyal
Dy. Managing Editor Soma B. Chowdhury
Design Consultant Shefali Upadhyay

First American Edition, 2014
Published in the United States by DK Publishing
345 Hudson Street, New York, New York 10014

14 15 16 17 18 10 9 8 7 6 5 4 3 2 1
001—197316—02/14

Copyright © 2014 Dorling Kindersley Limited
All rights reserved.Without limiting the rights under copyright reserved
above, no part of this publication may be reproduced, stored in or
introduced into a retrieval system, or transmitted, in any form, or by any
means (electronic, mechanical, photocopying, recording, or otherwise),
without the prior written permission of the copyright owner.
Published in Great Britain by Dorling Kindersley Limited.

A catalog record for this book is available
from the Library of Congress.

ISBN: 978-1-4654-1718-3 (pb)
ISBN: 978-1-4654-1918-7 (plc)

DK books are available at special discounts when purchased in bulk for
sales promotions, premiums, fund-raising, or educational use.
For details, contact:
DK Publishing Special Markets
345 Hudson Street, New York, New York 10014
SpecialSales@dk.com

Printed and bound in China
by South China Printing Company.

The publisher would like to thank the following for their kind
permission to reproduce their photographs:
a=above, b=below/bottom, c=center, l=left, r=right, t=top
1 **Dreamstime.com:** Isselee (br). 2 **Corbis:** Minden Pictures / JH
Editorial / Cyril Ruoso (tr); Imaginechina (cr); Keren Su (br).
3 **Corbis:** Katherine Feng. 4 **Corbis:** Minden Pictures / ZSSD. 5 **Pearson
Asset Library:** Jon Barlow / Pearson Education Ltd. 6 **Getty Images:**
Lonely Planet Images / Richard Nebesky. 7 **Corbis:** Imaginechina.
8-9 **Getty Images:** AFP / Roslan Rahman (b) 9 **Corbis:** Xinhua Press /
Chen Xie (tr). 10 **Corbis:** Karen Kasmauski. 11 **Corbis:** Minden Pictures
/ Katherine Feng. 12-13 **Getty Images:** AFP / Alain Jocard.
14 **Getty Images:** AFP / Ed Jones. 15 **Fotolia:** Michael Flippo.
16 **Corbis:** Imaginechina. 17 **Corbis:** Reuters / San Diego Zoo / Ken
Bohn. 18 **Corbis:** Xinhua Press / U.S. National Zoo (clb, crb).
19 **Corbis:** Xinhua Press / U.S. National Zoo (bl, br). 20 **Corbis:** Reuters.
21 **Corbis:** Minden Pictures / Katherine Feng. 22 **Corbis:** Minden
Pictures / Katherine Feng. 23 **Getty Images:** China Photos. 24 **Getty
Images:** Asahi Shimbun. 25 **Fotolia:** Eric Isselee. 26 **Getty Images:**
Stringer / China Photos. 27 **Getty Images:** ChinaFotoPress. 28 **Corbis:**
Minden Pictures / ZSSD. 29 **Dreamstime.com:** Roman Milert. 31 **Getty
Images:** ChinaFotoPress. 32 **Dreamstime.com:** Isselee (cra);
Fotolia: Eric Isselee (clb); **Getty Images:** China Photos (tr);
Getty Images: a.collectionRF / twinmist (br).
All images © Dorling Kindersley Limited
For further information see: www.dkimages.com

Discover more at
www.dk.com

DK READERS

BEGINNING
TO READ ALONE
2

THE GREAT PANDA TALE

CITY
ZOO

Admits one

Issue date :

Written by Laura Buller

Do you love learning about and meeting animals?

I am Louise and, since I was a little girl, the zoo has been my favorite place.

It is so exciting to see the animals up close and for real.

Roarrr!

I love to watch them move and play, and to hear them hoot, growl, and roar.
This year, I did the coolest thing ever.
I joined the Zoo Crew.
We are kids who help zoo visitors have a great day.

CITY ZOO

Zoo Crew volunteer
Name: Louise
Zoo Crew number: 00123

Being in the Zoo Crew
is so much fun.
Every day is different
from the last one.
Sometimes, we help
the zookeepers take
care of the animals.
On busy days, we work at
the ticket booth or the gift shop.
We never know what to expect!

The busy ticket booth

This summer, something
amazing happened.
We found out one of
our giant pandas was
expecting a baby.

It was big news for the zoo,
because no panda cubs had
ever been born there.

On the day we found out about
the baby, I was taking a package
to the head panda keeper,
Ms. Kelly.
I walked past
the panda enclosure to
the research center.
The enclosure is so beautiful.
It looks just like the pandas'
tree-covered home in China.
I spotted Gao Yun, the male
panda, but Zhen Mei, the female,
was nowhere to be seen.

Panda habitat

Wild pandas live high up in the mountains of central China. The forests are filled with bamboo plants and trees.

I could barely open
the doors when I reached
the research center.
The place was packed
with people.
I wove through the crowd.
Everyone was looking at the big
glass window into the lab.

Zhen Mei was there with
two animal doctors.
I was looking too and
bumped right into Ms. Kelly.
I asked her to tell me
what was going on.
She told me the vets were
doing tests on Zhen Mei.
They wanted to find out if
she was going to have a baby.

Birthday dates

A panda mother is
pregnant with her baby
for three to five months.
Babies are born in late
summer or early fall.

People were buzzing
with excitement.
A few minutes later,
one vet held her thumbs up
behind the window.

A huge cheer went up.
A new baby panda was
on the way!
This was fantastic news
for the whole zoo.

Pandas are
endangered animals.
There are only
a few thousand left
in the wild.
Zoos help pandas
to have babies
and research how to
protect wild pandas.

Over the next few months, we
took extra care with Zhen Mei.
My job was to help provide
her main meal: bamboo.
A panda chews through
a huge pile of bamboo every day.
Pandas need to eat lots of
bamboo to keep healthy.

One of the
zookeepers
pulling a
wagon of
bamboo for
the pandas

The zookeepers kept
a close eye on how much
Zhen Mei was eating.
They wanted to make sure
her baby was healthy and growing.
One vet did some tests on
her poop.
I wouldn't like to have that job!
Zhen Mei needed more time
away from the visitors, so they
built her a den.

Around July, we noticed
that Zhen Mei was eating
less bamboo.
She seemed to want to be alone
in the den almost all the time.
Was it time for the baby
to be born?
The vets gave her lots of
different tests.

They used an ultrasound machine
to see the baby inside her.
Afterward, Ms. Kelly told me
that Zhen Mei's cubs looked
strong and healthy.
Cubs!
I couldn't believe it.
Our panda mom was going
to have twins.

First baby picture

An ultrasound is
a special picture of
a baby while still inside
its mother.

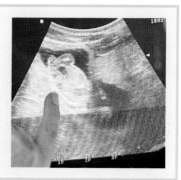

Over the next week, Zhen Mei seemed to spend almost all her time in her den.

The zoo team watched her on the panda cam, as she snoozed most of the day.

The vets thought this was a sign the twins were ready to be born.

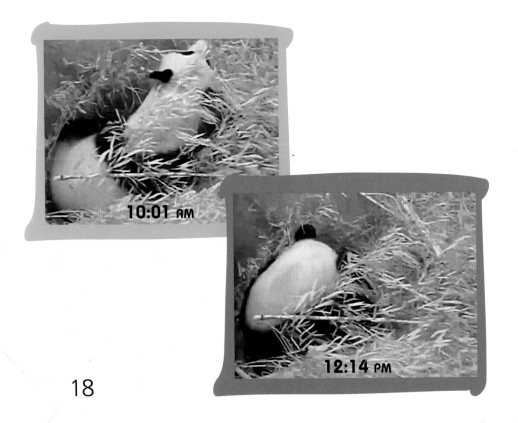

10:01 AM

12:14 PM

One morning, the zookeepers
heard a strange noise
from the panda enclosure.
They checked Zhen Mei.
They found her with
her new cubs.
The tiny babies were
crying for milk.
Soon the news spread
through the zoo.
The babies were here: a boy
and a girl!

4:20 PM

3:08 PM

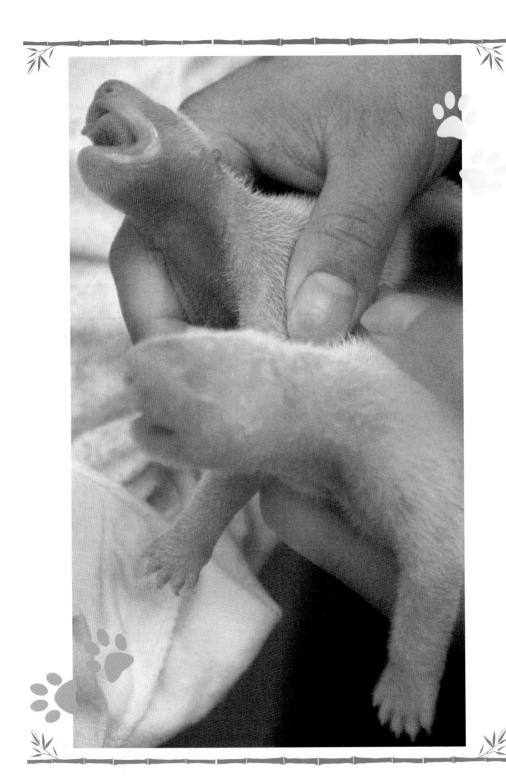

Tiny babies

At birth, a panda weighs only 3½ ozs (100 grams). No other mammal has babies so much smaller than the adult.

The panda cubs were tiny enough to cup in your hands.
They were a thousand times smaller than their mother.
They were pink and wrinkly, with a few patches of white hair on their bodies.
Every couple of hours, they cried to be fed.

The cubs' eyes were
squeezed shut.
They spent most of their time
sleeping and feeding.
This was just like me when
I was a newborn.
Zhen Mei hardly ever put
the babies down.
She cradled them in
her big panda paws.
She sometimes popped one
in her mouth.

The zookeepers made sure
both babies were getting
enough to eat.
They had a lot of growing
to do!
Each cub drank milk
from a bottle.
You could see a row of
tiny white teeth when they opened
their hungry mouths.

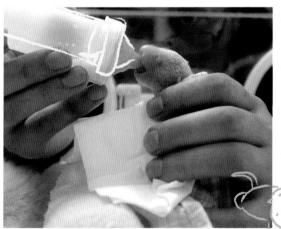

A newborn panda
is smaller than the
zookeeper's hand!

The panda twins were nearly
six weeks old.
I watched them through
a glass window in their nursery.
They were so cute!
Patches of black fur had grown
around their eyes, ears,
shoulders, and little legs.
Their eyes were open now, too.

The zoo asked everyone
to choose names for
the new pandas on its website.
People voted for their favorites.
I really liked the winning names,
Little Cloud for the male
and Snowdrop for the female.
At two months old, the cubs
were crawling and would take
their first steps soon.

Panda names

In Chinese tradition, babies are named after 100 days. Pandas always have Chinese names. Snowdrop is Xuehua and Little Cloud is Xiao Yun.

Little Cloud and Snowdrop
began walking when they
were around four months old.
Little Cloud could even run
for a few steps.
Snowdrop sometimes climbed
on her mother's back for a ride.

**Coming soon:
baby pandas!**
On show in November.
Baby viewing hours:
11:30 AM to 1:00 PM

Both cubs followed
their mother everywhere.
They copied everything
she did, from climbing trees
to eating bamboo.
Soon, it would be time for
visitors to see the panda twins.

27

I remember the day Snowdrop
and Little Cloud joined
their mother in the enclosure.
I went to see how they were doing.
First, I spotted Little Cloud.
He was playing with some
bamboo on the jungle gym.
His sister was looking down
on him from above.
Next, I saw Zhen Mei.
She was keeping an eye
on everyone.
She wanted to keep her
babies safe.
Suddenly, she looked right at me,
and waved!

It was the most amazing end
to an exciting year.

Giant Panda Facts

A newborn panda is pink and tiny. Black patches appear on its skin after a few days.

After a month, the baby looks like a mini grown-up panda.

At 3–4 months, the cub can stand and walk.

A panda starts eating bamboo when it is 6 months old.

A cub leaves its mom when it is 2 years old.

A panda starts having babies between the ages of 4 and 8 years.

Index

DK READERS help children learn to read, then read to learn. If you enjoyed this DK READER, then look out for these other titles ideal for your child.

Level 3 African Adventure

Experience the trip of a lifetime on an African safari as recorded in Katie's diary. Share her excitement when seeing wild animals up close, joining the park rangers on their night game drives, and help track rhinos from the air in a helicopter.

Level 3 LEGO® Friends: Summer Adventures

Enjoy a summer of fun in Heartlake City with Emma, Mia, Andrea, Stephanie, Olivia, and friends.

5